Contents

What is Christmas?. 4

When do people celebrate Christmas? . 6

What do people do at Christmas?. . . . 8

What are Christmas lights like?. 10

What do Christmas decorations
    look like? 12

What food do people eat
    at Christmas? 14

How do people dress at
    Christmas time? 16

What stories do people tell
    at Christmas? 18

Who gives presents at Christmas? . . . 20

Quiz. 22

Glossary 23

Index 24

Answers to quiz 24

What is Christmas?

Christmas is a celebration.

It is a special time for many people.

Christmas is a special day for people who believe in **Jesus**.

They remember the day he was born.

When do people celebrate Christmas?

DECEMBER						
1	2	3	4	5	6	7
8	9	10	11	12	13	14
15	16	17	18	19	20	21
22	23	24	25	26	27	28
29	30	31				

Christmas Day is 25 December.

But Christmas time is more than one day.

People put up Christmas decorations early in December.

They go to Christmas parties and concerts all month.

What do people do at Christmas?

On Christmas Day, some people go to church.

They may spend the day with their families.

Some people sing Christmas songs
called carols.

What are Christmas lights like?

Candles at Christmas make a pretty light.

There are candles inside churches.

There are lights on **Christmas trees**.

There are lights on houses and buildings.

What do Christmas decorations look like?

wreath

bow

There are green Christmas **wreaths** and **Christmas trees**.

There are red **bows** on the wreaths.

There are coloured Christmas tree lights and **ornaments**.

There are decorations in the shape of stars and snowflakes.

What food do people eat at Christmas?

Some people have a special dinner on Christmas Day.

They may cook a turkey or a ham.

Some people make special biscuits for Christmas.

The biscuits can be shaped like bells, stars or trees.

How do people dress at Christmas time?

In some places, it is very cold at Christmas time.

People in those places wear warm clothes.

In other places, it is very hot
at Christmas time.

People there dress to stay cool.

What stories do people tell at Christmas?

The Christmas story tells how **Jesus** was born.

Some children act out this story in a **nativity play**.

Some people read a famous poem on the night before Christmas.

The poem tells about a visit from **Saint Nicholas**.

Who gives presents at Christmas?

People give each other presents at Christmas time.

Some children make a list of the things they want.

There are presents under the **Christmas tree**.

Who puts them there?

Quiz

What are these Christmas things called?

Look for the answers on page 24.

?

?

?

Glossary

bow
way of tying ribbon in loops

Christmas tree
special tree decorated for Christmas

Jesus
the baby whose birth is celebrated at Christmas

nativity play
play about the birth of Jesus

ornament
something pretty to put on a Christmas tree

Saint Nicholas
Father Christmas, or the person who brings presents at Christmas time

wreath
leaves or flowers made into a circle

Index

biscuits 15

bows 12, 23

candles 10

carols 9

Christmas trees 11, 12, 13, 21, 23

churches 8, 10

clothes 16

decorations 7, 12–13

Father Christmas 23

food 14

ham 14

Jesus 5, 18, 23

lights 10, 11, 13

nativity play 18, 23

ornaments 13, 23

parties 7

poems 19

presents 20, 21

Saint Nicholas 19, 23

stories 18

turkey 14

wreaths 12, 23

Answers to quiz on page 22

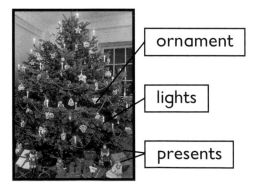

ornament

lights

presents

24